Buying Signals

How to spot the green light and increase sales

Nikki Rausch

YourSalesMaven.com

Buying Signals

This information is given to help you increase your sales. Results are stated as examples only and may not be typical. No guarantee written or implied comes with this information. It is however created with a genuine desire to help your business grow.

ISBN-10: 1-933750-13-8
ISBN-13: 978-1-933750-13-2

Buying Signals

Acknowledgements

My special thanks to Steve and Kathy Kidd for their support and guidance through this process. Writing one's second book seemed to be so much harder than the first. Thank you for your continued encouragement.

To Melina Young, your edits and suggestions were life savers. Thank you for your hard work and helping make this book so much better than I could have on my own.

This book is dedicated to Lesa Say. Lesa, it is because of your encouragement and support that I'm following my passion. My business and this book would not exist without you kindly pushing me to pursue it. I'm forever grateful to you. You are a blessing in my life.

Foreword

Buying signals are something we all see every day in business, and yet we can so easily miss them. Think about the times we have all said things like, "I don't know why they didn't buy." or "I *really* thought they were going to buy."

When looking back on a missed sales opportunity we tend to ask ourselves, "Why didn't they buy?" or "What did I miss?" and of course, "What could I have done different?" We especially find ourselves pondering questions like these when we think we should have made a sale.

Wouldn't it be great if everyone who wanted our product had a sign saying, "I want to buy!"

The reason I love the content in this book is because it contains the shocking news that our customers actually *do* have signs saying they want to buy. And we've been missing the BUYING SIGNALS.

Customers give us signals. They may not be, "Hey! Let me buy your stuff!" But in many ways, the things they do and say mean exactly that.

We know how to build relationships with people so they like, admire, and trust us. We know we have a product they want and need. Maybe we even thought they were going to get it ... and ... then ... they didn't.

By reading this book we can learn how to not miss these signals anymore. We'll learn how to recognize the buying signals our customers are giving.

I strongly encourage you to get ready for an explosive next level as you learn how to not miss the BUYING SIGNALS you are receiving ever again!

~Steve Kidd, Host of *Thriving Entrepreneur.*

Contents

Introduction 11

1. Why Learn About Buying Signals?......15

2. What's a Buying Signal?.....................25

3. Seventeen Buying Signals 29

4. What if You're Not Sure? 63

5. What's at Risk if You Miss the Buying
   Signal? 77

6. What Should I Say When I've Received a
   Buying Signal?..................................87

7. The Most Surprising Things About
   Buying Signals..................................99

8. Putting it into Practice Right Now!....105

Buying Signals

Introduction

My name is Nikki Rausch. I'm an author, speaker, trainer, and award-winning sales executive with 20 years of sales experience selling to organizations such as Bill & Melinda Gates Foundation, Johnson & Johnson, Hewlett Packard, Seattle Public Schools, and NASA. The majority of my sales experience comes from the technology industry – audio/visual in particular. In addition, I am a master certified practitioner of Neuro Linguistic Programming (NLP)[1] with over 1,200 classroom hours, either as a student, an assistant, or a trainer. In 2013, I combined my sales experience with my NLP background and started my own company, Sales Maven. I coach and train on

---

[1] NLP studies the pattern or "programming" created by the interaction between the mind ("neuro"), language ("linguistic") and the body.

communication and selling skills for sales professionals and business owners. I teach how to make authentic connections with clients, increase rapport, and ultimately be able to ask for the sale without being pushy or fearing rejection. Knowing how to communicate with your clients, recognize buying signals, and ask for the sale are crucial to the success of your business.

A couple of years ago, as the events director for a training organization in Washington, I began attending local networking events. At these events, I was observing a lot of conversations. I would often hear people give buying signals, but the other person completely missed the opportunity to ask for the sale. It was then that I realized, "Wow, I could really help people increase their sales!"

The realization that came from those networking events was the catalyst to write this book. Learning to recognize buying signals and knowing what to say when you get one will improve the communication between you and your client. It moves you from "we're just having a casual conversation" to "we're actually doing business together."

I have made it my mission to teach people more effective ways to build rapport, communicate, sell, and grow their businesses.

If you would like to grow your business by learning some simple tips and tricks that will allow you to recognize and make use of the buying signals you get every day, I invite you to continue reading.

Buying Signals

1. Why Learn About Buying Signals?

It's crucial to your success as a business owner to know 1) how to recognize a buying signal and 2) what to say after you receive one from a potential client. You can have the best product in the world. You can have the most value-packed offer there is. And if you don't have selling skills, it's all for naught.

The truth is, no matter what your job title is or what industry you're in, some aspect of your job includes interacting with other people. You may have the strongest business plan or the best product, but if you do not know how to sell or ask for a sale, chances are you'll be the best kept secret around. (And no one wants that.) Whether you see yourself as a salesperson or not, there's a selling component to doing business. Being an effective communicator and knowing how to sell will serve you.

A lot of times people in more passive industries think they can opt themselves out of identifying as a salesperson.

Whatever your industry, you have to be willing to invite people to do business. An often overlooked fact is, many people will not give you their business – unless you ask.

Even when they want to do business with you, people like to be asked. I love when somebody wants my business and is willing to step up and ask me. Many times, I won't make a decision until someone asks for my business. Even if I am not interested now, I may be interested down the road, and I will remember the person who cared enough to ask.

You can ask in a kind, authentic, and professional way. You don't have to be pushy or aggressive. You can be conversational. However, you do have to say the words and invite people to do business with you.

I love interacting with people who've honed their skills – those who take their profession seriously. The best telemarketers are the ones where you think, "Oh, I feel this person is genuinely interested in me," and they come across as being authentic. It doesn't feel like they're reading from a script or, regardless of what you say, they already have a rebuttal locked and loaded.

The best telemarketers understand it's about relationships. Likewise, you and I are in a conversation. We're in a relationship right now as you read this book. So it's important you know I'm invested and interested in offering you something of value to help you in your business. By offering you value, you'll keep reading. And at some point, you may even decide for us work together. It's about moving our relationship forward step by step to ultimately earn your business.

We tend to buy from people whom we know, like, and trust. If we don't like a person, it's unlikely we'll buy from them.

How many times has someone walked out of a business because they weren't treated well, received poor customer service, or felt like the salesperson was more interested in getting their money than solving their problem or meeting their need?

I've done this.

How many times have you walked into a place of business with the intent to purchase, and felt like the salesperson or the person behind the counter wasn't interested in helping you at all?

Maybe they weren't even rude, maybe they simply came off as distant or preoccupied. Whatever the circumstance, it gave you the sense they couldn't have cared less if you were there or not.

And how many times have you turned around, walked out, and thought, "Well, I'll either buy some other time, or I'll go down the street and give my money to someone else."

These days, there are plenty of options and places to spend your money – whether it's something as simple as buying a gallon of milk or as advanced as buying a car or a house. For every one person you consider doing business with, there are plenty of other people you could work with who do the same thing. So why deal with someone who isn't ready or invested in earning your business?

One way to set yourself (and your business) apart is to be interested in solving a problem, and meeting the need of your client. It bears repeating: **people buy from those they know, like, and trust**.

When you use rapport-building skills to increase your likeability and credibility, it leads to clients trusting you – and you earning their business.

When you learn to connect in an authentic way with clients, you make it easy for them to say yes. You become their first and only choice as the person to meet their need or solve their problem. They won't be interested in doing business with anybody else, because they like and trust you.

I know I'm willing to pay higher prices to continue to work with a person I like, trust, know and is invested in me. I would much rather work with them than go down the street and give my business to someone I don't have a relationship with who charges a few dollars less.

How about you? Do you always go for the least expensive option or are you willing to pay a little bit more for good customer service?

Chances are, you have your favorite vendors too. These are people you buy from on a regular basis and you've built a relationship with. You're loyal to them. So I must ask, do you present your business so your clients want to be loyal to you?

The whole idea is building long-term client relationships so you're successful in sales, in business, and in life. My success has been built on long-term client relationships. For me, the relationship comes first, and the sale is a byproduct of that relationship.

This is what I want for you and your business too! To build long-term client relationships where you are your clients' first and only choice.

When you can build a solid foundation which says, "I care about you," you'll bridge the gap between considering and buying – and find people coming to you, wanting to do business.

We should be as passionate about being genuine and real with our clients as we are about whatever it is we sell.

And this is why we need to recognize and act on buying signals!

Buying Signals

2. What's a Buying Signal?

A buying signal is an indication from your prospective client that they are interested in your product/service – and it's important to be on the lookout for them. You want to be paying attention so you're ready to act on a signal when you receive it. Why? Because the moment you receive a buying signal is the best time to invite someone to do business with you. Are you doing this as well as you could?

If not, the crucial step you might be missing today is, **you actually have to say the words and ask someone for their business**.

If this seems difficult or scary to you now – not to worry.

I am confident that after learning the buying signals, how to recognize them, and what to do when you get one...you'll no longer feel it's acceptable to hand someone your card and hope they'll call you.

So, what do they look like?

A buying signal can be as obvious as someone coming up and saying, "Hey, can I buy from you?" And, chances are, you don't need to read a book to recognize such an obvious buying signal.

However, many times the signals are more subtle.

A buying signal can be a verbal or non-verbal way for clients to let you know they're potentially interested in doing business with you.

Unfortunately, clients aren't usually so transparent to say things like, "Please take my money" or "Please let me buy from you." Therefore, it is necessary to identify and understand the murkier signals you are getting every day.

Learning the nuances of the more subtle buying signals I outline in this book will give you the confidence to invite clients to do business with you.

Once you have completed this book, you might find yourself saying things to yourself like, "Oh, I need to pay attention here, because this person may have just given me a buying signal."

And, if you aren't a natural salesperson, don't fret. I provide a lot of tips throughout the book to help you get more comfortable with this aspect of your business.

One key to help you make the transition to asking for sales – especially if it isn't something you identify with automatically – is knowing it's your job to invite clients to do business with you.

It's not the job of your client to beg you to let them work with you.

Why else is it important for you to know what buying signals are and what to do when you get them?

Simply put, understanding the buying signals your clients are giving you will help you provide better service to them. And, isn't that the whole point?

3. Seventeen Buying Signals

I have attended a *lot* of networking events. Over the years, I've compiled a list of different buying signals I watched people miss again and again.

This information helped build my business – I speak and train on buying signals quite a bit. In fact, it is the #1 topic people follow up with me on after my classes or sessions. They are overflowing with joy, excited to share how they booked new clients by putting what they learned into practice. (Which is something I love to hear about!)

As we go through these specific buying signals, don't be surprised if you find yourself thinking, "Oh!! I didn't realize that was a buying signal."

You may be surprised how often people are giving an opening for you to invite them to do business with you. As I've mentioned before, people like to be asked for their business.

So let's start with the top 17 buying signals.

(Note: I am aware some of these seem painfully obvious when you read them, but you would be surprised how often they are missed.)

Buying Signals

1. Asking about a specific product or type of service you offer
2. Asking about pricing
3. Asking about payment options or payment plans
4. Asking about the start of service or delivery
5. Asking you to repeat information you've already covered

6. Asking about next steps in the process of working with you

7. Asking what options are available

8. Asking for references

9. Asking for a discount

10. Asking about results and what to expect

11. Asking another person's opinion

12. Asking about what other clients have experienced when working with you or using your product

13. Making positive comments

14. Bringing up a negative experience with a previous provider

15. Asking "why" or "how" people work with you

16. Taking out his/her calendar, credit card, or other form of payment

17. Taking notes when you're sharing about your product/service

Again, I hope you looked over this list and thought, *"These seem pretty obvious."* That goes to show how easy it should be to start picking up on them, right? Maybe. The truth is, many of these signals are missed so often by business owners it would shock you.

Why is that?

The #1 reason these buying signals are missed is because they don't often come in such an obvious way--and more importantly--**the business owner does not act on the signal**.

If you're waiting around for your client to beg you to take their money, you'll be waiting a long time. And, you are missing business.

Let's talk about each buying signal individually to ensure you have clarity about each one by the end of this chapter.

1. Asking about a specific product or type of service you offer

Once someone asks a question about your product/service, it's important you do more than just answer the question. You then need to ask if they'd like to place an order or schedule a time to work with you. Many times, people answer questions about their product/service and then wait for the client to say they want to buy. (Insert crickets here.)

If you find yourself doing this, you're missing the buying signal.

Every time you get a buying signal, you need to invite the person to do business with you. And, yes, I do mean every time. I will give examples of why later in this chapter.

2. Asking about pricing

Here's one where you may be thinking to yourself, "Duh, this one's so obvious, I'd never miss it." And I hope you're right. But, let me give you an example of this where it isn't quite so obvious.

I had a client call me out of the blue one day wanting advice on how to handle a situation in a networking group we participate in. She shared how on two separate occasions a woman in the group came up to her after her 30-second elevator pitch with a hand on her hip and a particularly aggressive tone of voice, asking, "How much do you charge for your service?" My client shared how she was feeling judged by this woman and didn't quite know how to respond. She felt the woman in the group was demeaning her in some way by her body language and tone when she asked about her pricing. My response? "This sounds like a buying signal. Have you asked her to schedule a time to work with you?" My client was shocked at what I said. In an incredulous voice she said, "Nikki, you should hear the way she asks the question."

I explained, "One of two things will happen when you invite her to schedule a time to work with you, she'll either become a client or she'll stop asking what you charge. It's a win-win either way for you. You'll have a new client or you can spend your time connecting with other prospective clients at the event."

Fast forward a month and the woman with the tone stands up at our networking event raving about my client and the service she received. Turns out, it was a buying signal. She was simply waiting to be asked.

3. Asking about payment options or payment plans

A common way people will give you this buying signal is by saying something like, "So, how do people usually pay for your service?" The question is phrased as if they're asking for someone else. Chances are, what they really want to know is how they can pay you for your service. It's your job to answer the question and then invite them to do business with you. You might say, "I have two payment options available..." Outline the plans and then say, "Which option do you prefer?"

4. Asking about the start of service or delivery

When people are asking questions such as, "How long does it take from the time someone places an order with you before they receive their product?" it's a buying signal. Again, it sounds like they're asking for someone other than themselves. It's more likely they are thinking about placing an order with you.

To address this buying signal, answer the questions and then say, "Should we go ahead and get it ordered for you so you have it next week?"

5. Asking you to repeat information you've already covered

Clients ask you to repeat information for a few reasons: 1) they didn't hear you the first time, 2) they don't remember what you said, 3) they need clarification on the information you gave, or 4) they are creating an image in their mind of how they'll be using your product/service and want to get the details clear. In any case, this may be a buying signal.

When you find yourself repeating information, it's time to invite the client to do business with you.

6. Asking about next steps in the process of working with you

This buying signal often comes in the form of a question like, "So when someone signs up to work with you, what happens next?" Again, it can sound like they have someone else in mind when they're asking. In reality, they likely have questions about working with you and maybe aren't sure how to phrase them.

Nobody wants to sound "dumb" and when asking questions, we often worry we'll come across as unintelligent. It's your job to make it easy for the client and to let them know each question is important and valid.

In this case, explain the steps clients experience when buying your product or hiring your services and then invite them to do business. You might say, "The process of working with me is...[insert explanation]. Is this something you might be interested in doing?"

7. Asking what options are available

This buying signal is usually missed by the business owner because they answer the questions about options and then leave it there.

This is not the way to act on the buying signal. Instead, when a client asks which options are available, you answer the questions and then you ask, "Which option do you prefer?" By asking this follow-up question, you've now invited the client to do business with you in a "non-pushy" way. It's a simple question back to the client (and an invitation at the same time).

8. Asking for references

It's an excellent sign when a client asks you for a reference. I encourage you to have references on stand-by willing to speak about their experience of doing business with you.

When a client asks for references, you provide them and then invite them to move to the next step in the process. Maybe you need to schedule a follow-up call. You might say, "Should we go ahead and get a time on our schedules to circle back on this after you've had time to chat with my references?" Then give them a few dates and times.

It's so much easier to continue the conversation and move towards actually doing business together when you've scheduled your next step.

If you allow the conversation to end without getting a time scheduled to chat again, you'll likely find yourself in a phone tag spiral to nowhere. You also open the door for the prospective client to forget to reach out to your references. The more time goes by, the less likely you are to close the business.

9. Asking for a discount

Here's one of my favorite buying signals! Many business owners worry if a client asks for a discount and they tell them "no," they'll lose the sale.

This has rarely been the case in my experience.

Even when a client asks for a discount and you decline, you should still invite them to do business with you.

We have a culture of consumers programmed to expect discounts, sales, or clearance options. It's common practice for people to ask for a discount. I mean, it never hurts to ask, right?

When a client asks you for a discount and you are unable or unwilling to offer one, assume they want to buy from you and ask for their business.

I had a client call me frustrated because a customer had scheduled an appointment with her and a few days before the appointment sent an email asking for a discount. The customer had a list of reasons why she was asking for a discount. She mentioned her hours had been cut back at her job, she saw an ad for a competitor offering a lower price, and her husband was concerned about her spending money on the services.

When I asked my client if she wanted to offer a discount, she said, "No, I hate to lose her business, however, I can't afford to offer what she's asking for."

We crafted an email response where my client expressed how excited she was to work with the customer and all the benefits she'd receive at her scheduled appointment. She encouraged her to keep her appointment and if for some reason she was unable to, to please cancel within 48 hours.

Not only did the customer keep her scheduled appointment, she ended up purchasing a much bigger package than she'd originally planned for. And, the customer asking for the discount turned out to be the largest individual order my client has received yet.

So, when clients ask for a discount, even if you are unwilling to provide one, take the chance and invite them to do business with you.

You might be surprised at how often you still earn the business simply by asking.

10. Asking about results and what to expect

When clients ask about results, it's an indicator they are future pacing – imagining what it'll be like to have your product/service. Note, sometimes these buying signals are extremely subtle.

For instance, I had a woman once tell me she had no idea what it would be like to have a strategy call with me or how someone would even go about scheduling one. I explained the purpose of a strategy call and then said, "Most people schedule strategy calls with me while we're chatting about them. What do you think, should we go ahead and schedule one for you now? I keep my calendar right here on my phone. Do you have your calendar available?"

I then waited as she pulled out her phone, opened her calendar, and we scheduled a strategy call.

11. Asking another person's opinion

How many times have you had a client tell you they couldn't make a decision because they had to talk to their husband, wife, boss, or business partner? A lot of my clients tell me they assume this is a customer's way of giving them the brush off. Of course, maybe a brush off happens from time to time. However, you should still invite them to do business with you.

Here's what you might say in these instances, "I understand you need to speak with your [fill in the person they mentioned], when do you think you'll have a chance to chat with them? Let's go ahead and schedule a follow-up call now to close the loop on this after you've had a chance to speak with them." Schedule a follow-up appointment right then, in the moment.

The client now has a particular time limit to have the discussion, which creates a sense of urgency. They know you'll expect to discuss it again in a few days, so they better be ready. It's much more effective to already have the next step scheduled than waiting and hoping for them to call you back.

Even if they want to do business with you, waiting on them to take the next step will add unnecessary time and energy to earning their business. Having the appointment to finalize a decision on the calendar allows you to move forward, spending time and energy on your next client.

12. Asking about what other clients have experienced when working with you or using your product

It's helpful for many clients to get a sense of what to expect when they hear about what others have experienced when working with you. It's a way to put their mind at ease and reaffirm they're making a good decision. Have stories and concrete examples to share based on your previous clients' experiences. Again, answer the question and then invite them to book an appointment with you or place an order.

13. Making positive comments

This is probably the most overlooked buying signal I come across. When someone goes out of their way to give you a compliment about your product/service, be appreciative and then invite them to do business with you.

Let me give you an example.

About a year ago, I met a lovely woman at a networking event and we set up a date to meet for coffee. While at coffee she asked me about what services I offer at my company, Sales Maven.

When I shared what I do she said, "That's so interesting, I know a few people who would benefit from working with you."

"Ding, ding, ding!" (That is the sound I hear in my mind when I am presented with a potential buying signal.)

My response to her was, "Thank you. I would so appreciate if you'd be willing to make an introduction to the people you think would benefit from my work." I then said, "Now, how about you, is this something you might be interested in as well?" Her response was, "Nikki, I've been in sales for 20 years, I don't need help with sales." The conversation then shifted to another topic.

A few weeks later, she registered for one of my complimentary tele classes, which I offer about once a quarter.

Afterwards, she reached out to me and said, "Nikki, I didn't think I could learn anything new about sales and yet I did in your class.

Your approach is so different than traditional sales training I've had in the past." Positive comment – *ding, ding, ding*! A possible buying signal.

I thanked her for her compliment and then invited her to sign up for my signature program, Savvy Selling (a 5-week tele class I teach a few times a year). Her response was, "I don't really think a tele class is for me. However, I might like to work with you privately."

We scheduled a session and at the end of the session she said, "Wow, I got a lot out of today and I think there's more I could learn from you." *Ding, ding, ding.*

I invited her again to participate in the Savvy Selling class where I'd be teaching what she said she wanted to learn. She proceeded to tell me she wasn't interested in a class and would prefer to continue to work with me privately.

I offered to schedule another appointment with her and she said since it was summer she wanted to wait until the fall due to her busy travel plans.

A few months later she showed up at a class I was teaching for a networking group on sales. She sat in the front row directly in front of me. And, it just so happened the training I taught that night was the same training I offered a few months back on the free tele class she participated in.

Wow, now the heat was on.

I'd better be good because she's already heard this (of course, I always ensure every person in the room's engaged and learning something useful – this simply provided additional pressure to perform).

At the end of the training, as I was chatting with some people from the audience, the woman came over and stood a few feet away and waited to chat with me. The first thing she said to me was, "Nikki, I want to learn to speak like you." *Ding, ding, ding*, positive comment and a potential buying signal.

I said, "Thank you, that's so kind. You know my Savvy Selling class is about to start and in this class I teach a whole section on language skills. You're warmly invited to be a part of this group." She told me she'd started a new job and didn't have time for a tele class. I offered to work with her privately and she declined.

Later, when I arrived back to my office, I had an email from her which said, "I can't stop thinking about what I learned from you tonight and I want more. I'm in for Savvy Selling. Call me tomorrow and I'll give you my credit card to pay the tuition."

Let's review. Every time she made a positive comment, I invited her to work with me. She told me "no" multiple times before she ever said "yes." And that's ok. I was willing to build the relationship and invite her to do business every time I heard a buying signal (see, I told you an example of this was coming).

In case you're curious, she's a very happy client and still raves about what she learned in Savvy Selling. We all have a certain number of times we say "no" before we say "yes."

Be willing to invest in the relationship with prospective clients. And when they give you a buying signal, kindly invite them to do business with you – even if they have said no to you in the past.

14. Bringing up a negative experience with a previous provider

A few years back, I was asked to be the keynote speaker at a company's national sales convention. One of the topics I spoke about were five key buying signals, and this one was on the list. There were 90+ sales professionals in the room and when I put the slide up on the screen stating how bringing up a negative experience with a previous provider is a potential buying signal there was a collective groan in the room.

When I asked why they were groaning they said things like,

"That's the worst!" "I hate it when that happens." And, "I never know what to say."

I asked them to hear me out and I explained when people bring up a negative experience, they're looking for you to reassure them in some way about how working with you will be different. Be willing to stay in the conversation. You might say, "I'm so sorry you had a bad experience in the past. If you'd be willing to consider working with me, I can assure you your experience this time around will be much different and here's how..." Now tell them what you do with clients and share a story or two about what others have experienced when working with you. Make sure your examples demonstrate a positive experience that counters what they went through in the past with the other provider.

Next, invite them to do business with you.

You may be surprised at how often people are willing to give you a shot when you reassure them of how you'll take care of them.

15. Asking "why" or "how" people work with you

This is a relatively new buying signal I started teaching. I added it to the list after attending an event and having a particular conversation with a woman I met there. The event was a social hour and people were mingling around. A woman came up and read my name tag and said, "Sales Maven, what's that?" I gave her a short answer about what I do.

Her response was, "Why would anyone need help with sales?" Not only did her question come across quite direct, her tone of voice led me to believe she thought it was ridiculous.

The immediate thought that came to mind was, "Wow, how rude!" My next thought was, "What would I tell a client to do in this instance?"

So, I answered her question as I would for anyone wanting to know about the advantages of learning to be confident when selling.

After she heard my response, she said in a thoughtful tone, "Yes, I can see that, I often face those challenges myself." I then invited her to book a complimentary strategy call with me to discuss how we might work together.

The point is, even when people say things you might interpret as direct, harsh (or even rude), it's worth it to check and see if it's a buying signal. In this case, she declined the strategy session, however, I noticed she signed up on my website to receive my newsletter where a sales tip is offered each week.

16. Taking out his/her calendar, credit card, or other form of payment

When I hear someone say to a business owner, "I'd like to schedule a time to work with you" and the business owner hands the person a business card and says, "Give me a call and we'll get a time scheduled," I want to bang my head on a table.

This is one of the biggest crimes against buying signals and probably the one that hurts me the most. (Honestly, I can feel my soul dying a little when I witness it.)

When a client mentions scheduling a time to work with you, take out your calendar and schedule the appointment on the spot. When you hand someone a business card and say, "Call me," you risk never hearing from the person again.

It's not that the client loses interest per se, it's more likely because people get busy and distracted.

As soon as they're done talking to you they have voicemails to listen to, emails to return, social media to engage in, meal plans to finalize, kids to drive to soccer practice, and the list goes on and on.

You want to catch people when they're at the peak of their interest in working with you. And, I promise you, the moment they give you this buying signal is one of those times. Take the 90 seconds required to get them on your schedule or get their order placed. Remember, it's your job to make it easy for your clients to work with you.

I once told a woman I wanted to order her product. She gave me her business card and told me to call her next week. I was floored. She had a ready and willing customer and she blew me off.

Do you think I called her the following week? Nope. I waited until I met someone else selling the same product and gave my order to them. I ordered from a person ready and willing to take my business.

17. Taking notes when you're sharing about your product/service

The last on the list of buying signals may seem really obvious to you now as you're hopefully more aware of these *"Ding, ding, ding"* moments.

When a client takes the time to write down what you're saying, it's a huge buying signal. Make sure you pause and let them finish writing before you move on to your next point. Once you've finished your presentation, answered their questions, and they've stopped writing, wait for them to look at you and then invite them to do business.

Buying Signals

4. What if You're Not Sure?

At this point you may be asking, "How can I be sure it's a buying signal?" Or, "How do I know in a group environment whether the person is just being nice or if they're genuinely interested? How can I tell if the comment made or the question asked is a buying signal or someone trying to get rid of me?"

Here's how to uncover if you're receiving a buying signal: **you invite the person to do business with you**.

If the client says, "No, that's not for me," it's okay. Now the conversation can move on to something else.

In all of my years in sales, I have never invited anyone to do business with me and had the person be offended by my asking.

Sometimes, the person giving the signal may not yet realize they're interested in doing business with you. By inviting them to place an order or schedule an appointment, they can decide in the moment if they're ready to move forward.

Your chances of earning their business go up significantly simply by asking.

Any time there's even a hint of a buying signal, it's your duty to investigate (by inviting them to do business with you).

I know, this may be coming off like a broken record at this point, but the repetition is intentional. A lot of the tips in this book are simple – and if you are willing to take the actions I suggest, your business will benefit from it.

Many clients have told me this one tip of inviting and asking has transformed their businesses. I love getting feedback from clients saying how, "All of a sudden" they're signing up clients left and right – and how surprised they are it came from such a simple tweak to what they were doing.

So when it comes to buying signals, one rule trumps them all. I am guessing you could repeat it with me at this point, but here it is:

When you get a buying signal – Ask. For. The. Sale.

Yes, it's true, your product/service will not be a fit for everyone. And, yes, it's true, sometimes you will hear a few "no" responses before you get a "yes." However, asking often increases the number of opportunities you have to get a new client.

Let me give you an example. A few months back I spoke at a success conference for women in business. At the end of the event, the conference had set up expert tables for each of the speakers where the attendees could come over, sit down, and ask questions.

A woman sat at my table with a list of questions about sales. As I answered her questions, she was furiously writing my answers down in her notebook. *Ding, ding, ding! Potential buying signal.*

As she got up to leave, I turned to her and invited her to sign up for the Savvy Selling class. I said, "Based on these great questions you asked, you might consider registering for the Savvy Selling class where

I'll be going into much more detail on the topics we've discussed so far. What do you think, is this something you'd be interested in?"

She turned to me, put her hand on my arm and said, *"No."* I thanked her for her time and let her know how much I enjoyed connecting with her. This was important information in the moment because I was able to then turn my attention back to the others at the table to continue connecting and answering their questions. Turns out, three of the people at the table *did* sign up for Savvy Selling. The woman who told me "no" wasn't offended by me inviting her to do business and I didn't take her "no" personally. The "no" is information, not rejection.

I picked up a buying signal, I checked it out and it turned out she wasn't interested right then.

She's since connected with me on LinkedIn and Facebook. You never know – she may become a client down the road (or refer other clients to me). Whatever happens, you can be sure if she ever gives me another buying signal in the future, I will invite her to do business.

Now, I know, some of you may have read the last story and thought, "Oh man, I don't know if I can handle a straight 'No' like that...I'm not good at rejection and that feels pretty harsh."

Here's a little tip and some insight into how I view being told "No." (In whatever form it comes to me.)

In my mind, when someone tells me "No," I say to myself, "Not yet."

I also know there are many reasons people say, "No." (I dedicate a whole hour of the Savvy Selling class to getting told "No" and how to increase your chances of getting a "Yes.")

You need to be willing to keep the rapport going, stay connected, and look for opportunities to earn their business in the future.

Now, let's add another important step for setting yourself up for business now and in the future. This step involves paying attention and being a good listener. Let's face it, in order to recognize buying signals, you have to be listening for them. Buying signals are happening all the time, and sometimes in the most unlikely of places – so you've got to tune in.

As you begin to listen for buying signals, you may hear them while standing in line to buy a cup of coffee, during a family gathering, at a neighborhood party, or possibly from a parent at your child's school. Always be on the lookout and listening for the signals.

Let me take a minute to address what it means to be a good listener. That way, you'll be ready to start picking up the buying signals when you hear them.

First, there are four levels of listening. And, one of them is ideal for catching buying signals.

Level 1: Cosmetic Listening

Cosmetic listening is when you're in conversation with someone and they are either distracted or not paying attention to you.

We experience this level of listening frequently in our cell phone culture – with everyone checking their phones during conversation.

You know who I'm talking about. The people who say they "multitask" while talking to you. They're on Facebook, Twitter, or Instagram, and during the conversation you may get a lot of "uh huh" or "yeah, oh really." responses.

When you're listening at the cosmetic level you can be sure you're missing the buying signals.

Level 2: Conversational Listening

Conversational listening happens when we are listening just enough to be able to respond. We're waiting for our turn to share what we know about the topic.

It's almost like when you were in grade school at recess playing jump rope. Do you remember waiting for the perfect moment for the rope to swing around so you could jump in?

Conversational listening is a similar feeling, waiting for the perfect moment to jump in. You're more concerned with the perfect moment to jump rather than paying attention and connecting in an authentic way with the other person.

Conversational listening happens a lot at networking events, dinner parties, and other social functions where you're meeting people you might never see again. There's little investment in the conversation. Unfortunately, in these settings, buying signals are rampant and being missed like crazy.

Level 3: Active Listening

The third level is known as active listening. When you're actively listening, you're authentically giving your attention to the other person. You're setting aside any internal dialogue or thoughts which might interfere with you being completely engaged in the conversation.

Unlike conversational listening (when you're distracted and not able to actively listen) active listening means you shut everything else out and focus on the person and conversation in front of you.

This is the ideal state of listening for catching (and acting on) buying signals. Once you start actively listening, you'll discover how easy it is to pick up buying signals and invite people to do business with you.

Level 4: Deep Listening

Deep listening is usually reserved for trained professionals like therapists, grief counselors, and clergy.

Here's a graphic to help you remember all of
the levels:

It is important to spend time practicing
being a good listener--for your personal life
and your business. As you become a better
listener I'll bet you'll find more people
wanting to spend time with you and do

business with you. It will also make it easier for you to recognize buying signals and invite people to become clients.

5. What's at Risk if You Miss the Buying Signal?

What do you risk when you don't listen for and catch buying signals?

The obvious, of course, is you risk losing business. A less obvious risk, yet equally important, is you may damage the rapport and relationship with the prospective client.

Let me tell you what I mean...

Most of us walk around in our own little world and we think everything is about us. We tend to take things personally when something's said (or even left unsaid). Many of us think we're mind readers and decide what the other person "really" meant when they said that thing to us last week, or what they "actually" meant when they didn't say something else.

Has anyone ever approached you after you had a conversation and accused you of really meaning something else when you said whatever it was you said? Maybe you were surprised by the assumption they made. (And maybe you read a little more into what they really meant by asking you the question in the first place.)

Making assumptions are a part of human nature – we all do it. It is important to remember that prospective clients are people like everyone else. When you say things (or leave things unsaid) they will fill in the gaps by making assumptions. The important question to ask yourself is, will their story be better or worse than the truth?

Prospective clients may walk away from a conversation wondering why you didn't invite them to do business with you. They may feel unsatisfied in some way – or worse – they may assume you're not interested in doing business with them.

I have actually had people say to me: "I mentioned to so and so I wanted to buy his product and he never asked me for my business. I'm assuming he's not interested in selling to me."

When I check in with the business owner about the possible buying signal they typically respond with, "She gave me a buying signal? I had no idea!"

Potential clients make all kinds of assumptions. Here are a few common ones:

• "She's not interested in my business."
• "She doesn't think I'm a good fit for her product/service."
• "She's too busy to take on more clients."

• "She doesn't like me."

Chances are none of these assumptions are true. We'd love to do business with this prospective client, we just missed the buying signal.

Any time these assumptions are made, we risk damaging the relationship and losing out on earning future business.

Remember the woman I mentioned earlier who told me to call her next week to place an order? I assumed she wasn't interested in my business so I ordered from someone else.

In order to minimize these wrong assumptions, consider doing some preplanning before interacting with prospective clients. Set up an outcome or goal and commit to being an active listener.

Truly invest in the person with whom you're conversing.

Be mentally present in the moment. Not only will the person you're talking with appreciate you, you'll improve your chances of picking up a buying signal.

I spend quite a bit of time working with my clients setting up outcomes and managing their mental state before they attend networking events.

Contrary to popular belief/experience, the purpose of attending events isn't to hand out as many business cards as you can and hope someone calls you.

It should be about actively listening so you can build connections, develop relation-ships, and find out how you can solve a problem or meet a need for your prospective clients. And then, if you receive a buying signal or determine you can fit a need they have – invite them to do business with you.

If, after completing your reading, you find yourself saying, "Here's my business card, call me," you've missed the whole point of this book.

When you get to the core of it, the most important message of this book (the point) is: **Make it easy for people to do business with you**.

One way to do that is to act on buying signals at the moment they come to you.

It's actually much easier on both parties to close a sale, book an appointment, or schedule a follow-up conversation in the moment (when the prospective client is live in person, or on the phone with you).

Of course, there are times it doesn't make sense to ask for a sale in the moment. For example, if you need additional information from the client.

However, it may be appropriate to say, "What do you think about us scheduling a time to chat about this? Do you have your calendar available? Let's get an appointment on our books to follow-up with each other." Now, you've made it easy for them to do business with you.

Why? Keeping an already scheduled appointment is more convenient and takes less effort than calling you to cancel.

On the other hand, when you say: "Here's my card, call me," you're making it harder for clients to do business with you. It requires effort and planning to pick up the phone and schedule an appointment or place an order.

I meet people all the time that say, "You know, Nikki, I'd really like to get to know you. I'm wondering if we could set up a time to chat?" And I say, "Sure, let's get a time on our schedules now. Do you have your calendar available?" I know if I don't schedule a time on my calendar immediately, the chances of us actually getting together are slim to none. My schedule fills up quickly and I can only assume the other person's schedule fills up fast too.

If I want to get to know someone, I'll take the few extra minutes to get time scheduled on my calendar right then.

Bonus tip: I then ask if they have something in particular they'd like to chat about or if they're interested in doing business together (checking to see if they're giving me a buying signal).

Too many business owners push the responsibility of scheduling back onto the client. Often, these are the same business owners wondering why their sales are flat and why people aren't doing business with them.

In case you haven't figured this out on your own already...I'm going to let you in on a little secret. Most clients will not jump through hoops to work with you – and they shouldn't have to.

Buying Signals

6. What Should I Say When I've Received a Buying Signal?

When you think you hear a buying signal, do you know what to do next?

The simple answer is to invite the person giving the signal to do business with you. But let's explore your options a little more.

Remember, the goal is to make it as easy as possible for this prospective client to do business with you. So, one of the first things you can do is find out if what you just picked up on really *is* a buying signal. You might say, "I'm wondering if you'd like to know more? Should we schedule a time to chat further about this?"

These two simple questions will give the client an opportunity to decide and then tell you what they prefer the next steps to be. If they seem unsure, then it's a good idea to make passive suggestions. You might say, "I keep my schedule on my phone, how about you? We could get a time on our schedule now. That way I can be sure to answer any questions that come to mind for you."

Or, you might say, "I can get this information out to you and you can take a look at it, but let's still schedule a time to circle back in a few days. This way I can answer any questions you have or we can decide on best next steps." With this option, be sure to pick a specific time when you'll be connecting again. Get a time on your calendar for a call or a meeting.

A third option is to say, "This information might take a few days to get to you. I want to give you a couple of days to look at it, so let's schedule a time for a week or so out to circle back and decide on next steps."

Pulling out the calendars is a crucial step. If you leave your conversations open-ended with no additional time scheduled, saying something like, "Maybe we'll get back together," or "When you get it, let me know what you think," you risk never being able to get ahold of the person again. That could lead to spinning your wheels, wasting valuable time playing phone tag.

And, no matter how tempted you are to break the silence, be willing to stay quiet and wait after you say, "Let's get this on our schedules. Do you have your calendar available?" People are uncomfortable with silence, and so you know they will come up with an answer. Don't rush them (use your active listening skills). They will either say yes, no, or they'll tell you if they prefer something else. Whatever their response, it will let you know what to do next in your interactions with them.

If you are selling products, you may need to use different language. Perhaps something like, "Should we plan to have that delivered to you next week?"

When they're giving you a buying signal, and you ask the question above, it encourages people to tell you what they prefer. They may not even make a buying decision until you ask a question like, "Should we go ahead and get that ordered for you?"

Posing the suggestion causes them to ask themselves questions like, "Do I want to buy this?" or "What else do I need to know in order to make a decision?" Again, give them time to answer. Whatever their response, you'll know what to do next.

Think of these questions as a way for you to subtly check to see if you're on the right track. If it turns out it wasn't a buying signal or they're not ready to make a decision, keep the rapport going, and stay engaged in conversation. (Remember the example I gave of the woman I went back and forth with for months before she took action and decided to work with me).

Take the time to find out what else they need to make a decision. To do this, you may need to politely uncover some additional information. For instance, who else is involved in the decision-making process? What would be useful for them to know to be able to make a decision?

Here are the most common responses I use when I want to check and see if I'm getting a buying signal:

Possible Responses to Buying Signals:

1. "Would you like to go ahead and order that now?"

2. "Should we plan to have that delivered to you on...?"

3. "We can have that to you by (fill in the date). Should we plan for that?"

4. "I appreciate you asking for a discount, here's what I can do."

5. "Let's get an appointment scheduled, do you have your calendar available?"

A while back, I was speaking to a mastermind group and at the end they asked, "Ok, Nikki, how can we get more from you; how can people work with you?" I told them there are two main ways people work with me. First, I have my signature 5-week, Savvy Selling class. And, for people ready to dive deep into their business and hone their selling skills, I offer a 2-month VIP program.

There were five people in the mastermind group. Three of the five gave me buying signals by making comments like, "I would want your VIP program." One woman said, "I'm in" and I responded with, "Great, let's get your first session scheduled, do you have your calendar available?"

I hadn't even mentioned pricing before she scheduled her first session. Then she asked if I take credit cards, and I said I did. After handing me her card she said, "What's the fee for the VIP program?" It really didn't matter what the price was, she'd already decided I had something to meet her needs and solve her problems.

Yes, I am aware this is not always going to be the case. However, when people are totally focused on price it might be an indication you haven't demonstrated how your product/service meets their needs, solves their problem, or they don't yet see the value of your product/ service.

Of course, every once in a while you'll come across individuals who act like even if your product/service was five dollars, it'd be too much for them to spend. That's great information for you, and it teaches an important lesson: not everyone is your customer. Don't waste your time trying to convince people who will never want or need your services. Instead, focus your time and energy on people in need of your product/service and the kind of people you want to work with in your business.

My coach once told me, when people ask her for pricing she says, "Now I haven't actually heard from you yet whether or not this is something you're interested in." A statement like that puts it back on the person asking for pricing to reveal if they're really interested. There's no need to talk pricing if they're not interested.

To make the best of every conversation with a potential client you definitely need a plan. I teach my Savvy Selling class participants how to set up objectives before the start of a meeting to maximize their time and energy. Of course, objections come up and you need to be prepared to handle those. Learning to ask and answer questions is an important selling skill.

As sales people, sometimes we're afraid to ask questions because we think, "If I'm asking questions, clients might think I don't know what I'm talking about." This isn't true at all. Actually, it's the person asking the questions who holds the power in a conversation.

So, if you don't know the answer...ask.

It's also important when working with a client to leave time and space for them to ask questions as well. There needs to be a balance of power in the relationship to build rapport and deepen the level of communication. A great way to balance the power is for both of you to have time to ask questions of each other.

Now, how you ask your questions is also important. If clients feel like they're being interrogated, it isn't going to go over very well. However, if you ask in a kind, interested, and curious way, clients are more inclined to share information with you.

Lewis Carroll, the author of *Alice in Wonderland*, is quoted as saying, "If you don't know where you're going, any road will get you there." It is the same with clients. You need to know where you're going, have a plan, ask strategic questions, and help lead your client to the outcome that will be a win/win for all parties.

To recap, when you think you've received a buying signal:

1. Invite the client to do business with you using one of the possible phrases listed earlier in the chapter.

2. Be genuinely interested in the client to uncover their need/problem.

3. Have a plan for what you want to sell to them.

4. Don't be afraid to ask questions.

Buying Signals

7. The Most Surprising Things About Buying Signals

Clients regularly report how surprised they are to find buying signals showing up in all different ways, and in many different conversations.

It's more than the traditional client interactions, where you have a prospective client, you set up a time to meet so it makes sense, and there's a good chance you will encounter a buying signal during the conversation.

The less traditional interactions can come from anywhere or from anyone.

You never know who might be a prospective client. You should turn on your active listening skills and be on the lookout for these prospects – even in places where you would least expect them to be.

Here's an example of a buying signal showing up in an unlikely place. A client who runs a service-based business went to get her nails done. During her nail appointment the nail technician commented on my client's business. She said: "It must be really hard for you because people probably only come to see you one time. You must always be having to find new clients."

My client initially thought the technician was making small talk while doing her nails. After learning about buying signals she called me to ask if these types of comments were in fact a buying signal. I told her to check it out at her next nail appointment and invite the woman to schedule an appointment for services.

My client later reported that the technician *did* in fact schedule a session with her. Before learning about buying signals she never would have invited the nail technician to schedule an appointment. She would have assumed it was only small talk. She was there to get her nails done, and didn't have business on her mind.

That is precisely why I encourage you to be on the lookout for buying signals all the time. They show up in some of the least expected environments. Finding and acting on these unexpected occurrences can do wonders for your business.

Now, I know you won't get the exact same question in the exact same environment as this example, so here is what to be looking for: subtext. Or, what is the meaning beneath the actual words someone is saying to you?

Even though the comment in this example was in regards to how it must be hard for my client since she has a high turnover rate of clients, the real underlying question from the technician was, "How do I do business with you?"

When my client told her, "Actually, I have clients that work with me on a regular basis. Some come every month, some come every quarter, and some see me twice a year." And then she asked, "Is this something you might be interested in? We could schedule a session for you as early as next week."

The technician said yes and scheduled her first session.

My client could have taken offense to the way the comments were phrased or chalked it up to someone not understanding her business. Instead, she chose to check it out and it resulted in a new customer.

When someone makes a comment to you about your business – get curious.

Ask clarifying questions such as, "What specifically do you mean when you say it must be hard to always be finding new clients?" Or "I'm wondering, what makes you think that?"

My biggest advice to you is to always be on the lookout for buying signals and every time you receive one – investigate it. It may turn out the person who does your nails, your hair, or the person you've been friends with for 20 years actually has a need or a problem you can solve.

Unrecognized buying signals may be one of the biggest challenges in your business today. By learning to identify the signals and act on them, you could transform your business and watch your sales soar.

And, I'll say it again. When you're unsure, the easiest way to find out if what you picked up on really *was* a buying signal – is to **invite the person to do business with you**.

8. Putting it into Practice Right Now!

We covered a lot of tips and topics throughout this book. That being said, the #1 thing I recommend is to pay attention to the conversations you're having. Always be listening. Have a genuine interest in what people are saying to you, and don't be afraid to ask them to do business with you. If there's even a small chance it's a buying signal, assume it is and (all together now) **invite the person to do business with you**.

You will be surprised at how quickly your sales start to increase.

I wish you the best in your search for the "green lights."

Buying Signals

For anyone wanting more:

I warmly invite you to visit my website at
YourSalesMaven.com.

To connect on social media:

Twitter: *@yoursalesmaven*

Facebook: *facebook.com/yoursalesmaven*

LinkedIn: *linkedin.com/in/nicolerausch*

Instagram: *your_sales_maven*

To speak with me directly:

You are welcome to schedule a complimentary strategy call to find out how we might work together at *meetme.so/salesmaven.*

Also by Nikki Rausch:

Six-Word Lessons on Influencing with Grace: 100 Lessons to Genuinely Connect with Colleagues, Friends, Family and Lovers, available at *6WordLessons.com* in print and e-book.

Made in the USA
Middletown, DE
26 July 2018